The House in the Meadow

Shutta Crum

illustrated by Paige Billin-Frye

For the best carpenters and electricians I know,
my brothers, Calvin and John Crum.
S.C.

To Giliah
P. B-F.

*Inspired by the poem "Over in the Meadow"
by Olive A. Wadsworth.*

The House in the Meadow by Shutta Crum, illustrated by Paige Billin-Frye. Text copyright © 2003 by Shutta Crum. Illustrations copyright © 2003 by Paige Billin-Frye. Originally published in hardcover by Albert Whitman & Company. Used with permission. All rights reserved.

This version of *The House in the Meadow* published by Scott Foresman.

ISBN: 0-328-17016-X

All Rights Reserved. Printed in the United States of America. This publication is protected by Copyright, and permission should be obtained from the publisher prior to any prohibited reproduction, storage in a retrieval system, or transmission in any form by any means, electronic, mechanical, photocopying, recording, or otherwise. For information regarding permission(s), write to: Permissions Department, Scott Foresman, 1900 East Lake Avenue, Glenview, Illinois 60025.

3 4 5 6 7 8 9 10 V008 12 11 10 09 08 07

Over in the meadow, it was springtime when . . .

came a bride and a groom and their best friends **10**.
"And now…" said the couple. "A house!" said the **10**.
So they planned through the year, and when spring came again . . .

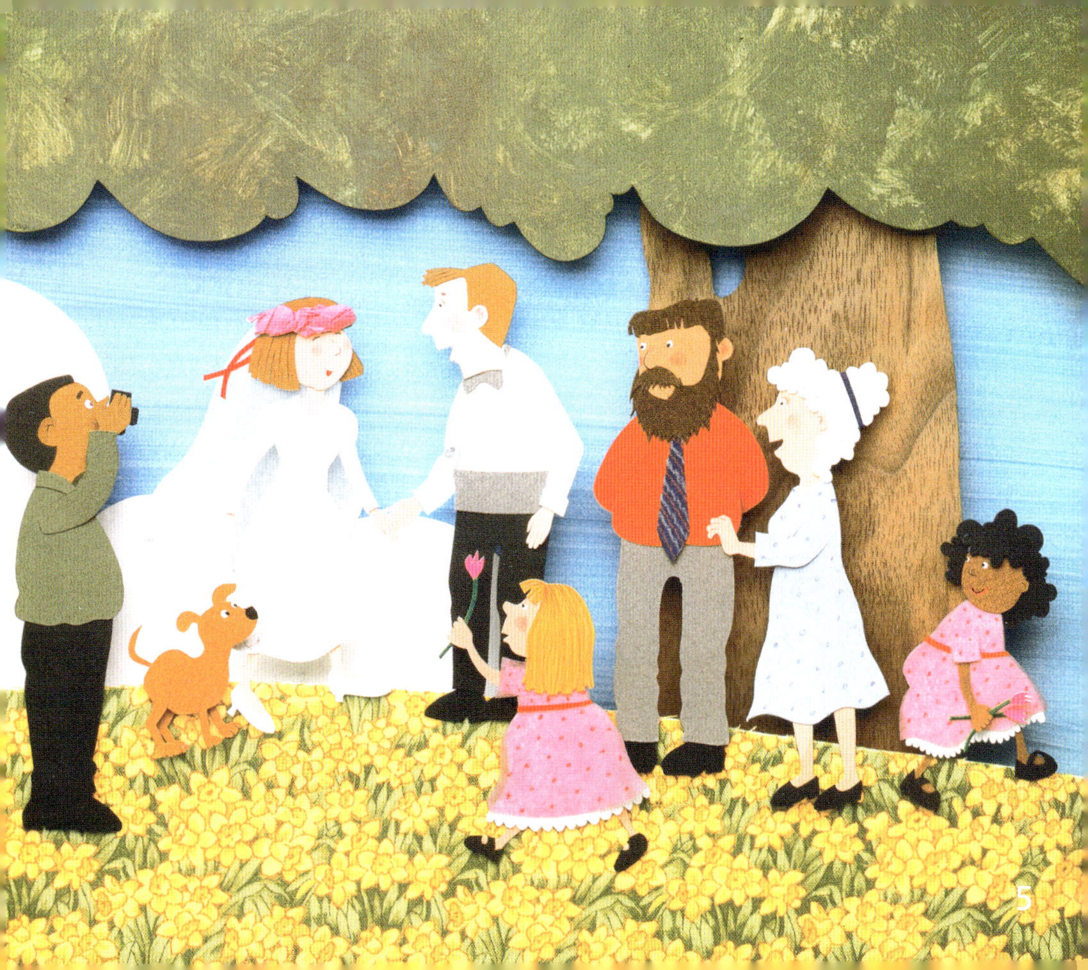

Over in the meadow, with a bucket big and fine,
shoveled Charlie with a backhoe and strong diggers **9.**

7

"Dig!" said Charlie. "We dig," said the **9.**
So they dug and dumped dirt with a bucket big and fine.

9

10

Over in the meadow, beside forms strong and straight,
Peter mixed concrete with his messy masons **8.**
"Pour!" said Peter. "We pour," said the **8.**
So they poured the concrete into forms strong and straight.

Over in the meadow, big carpenter Kevin
sawed up the lumber with his ready team of **7.**

13

"Build!" said Kevin. "We build," said the **7.**
So they built sturdy walls with carpenter Kevin.

15

Over in the meadow, at the spot marked with sticks,
worked Cindy with a rig and muddy drillers **6.**
"Drill!" said Cindy. "We drill," said the **6.**
So they drilled down for water at the spot marked with sticks.

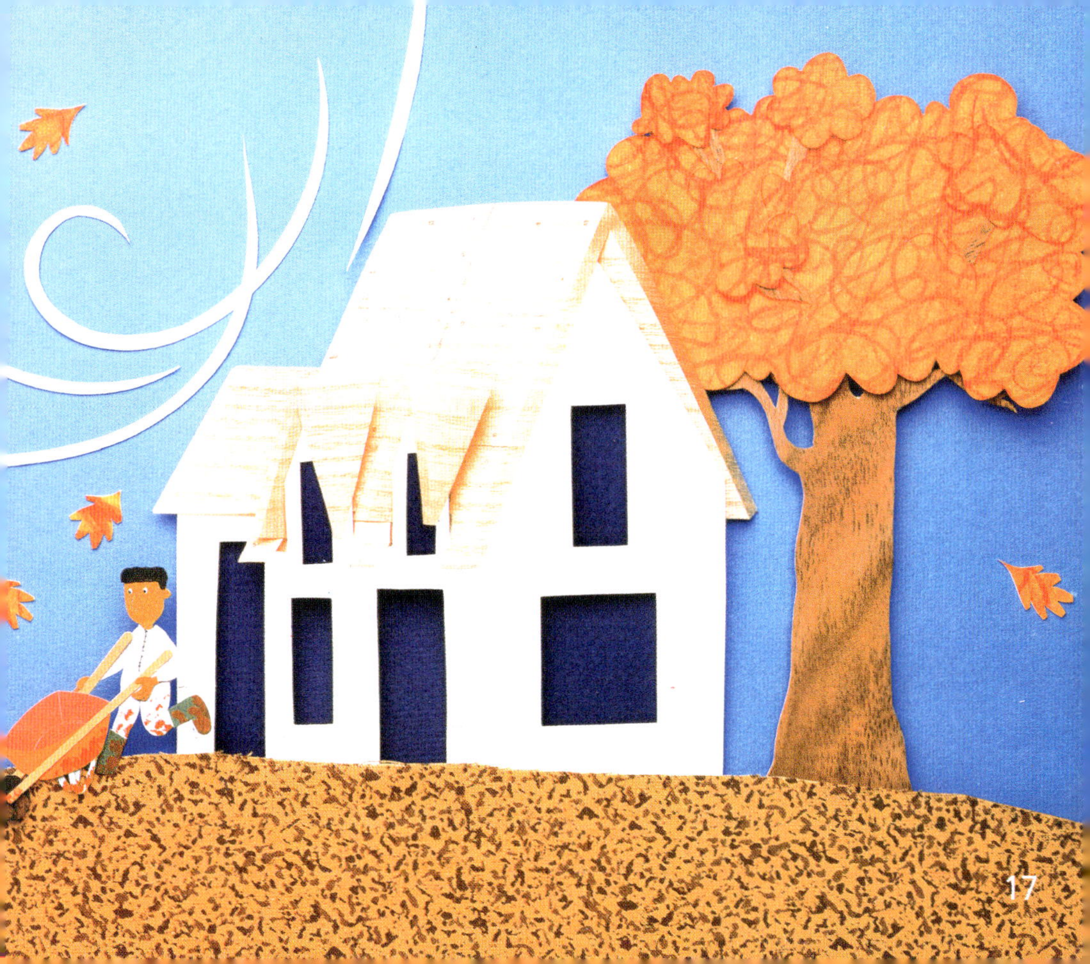

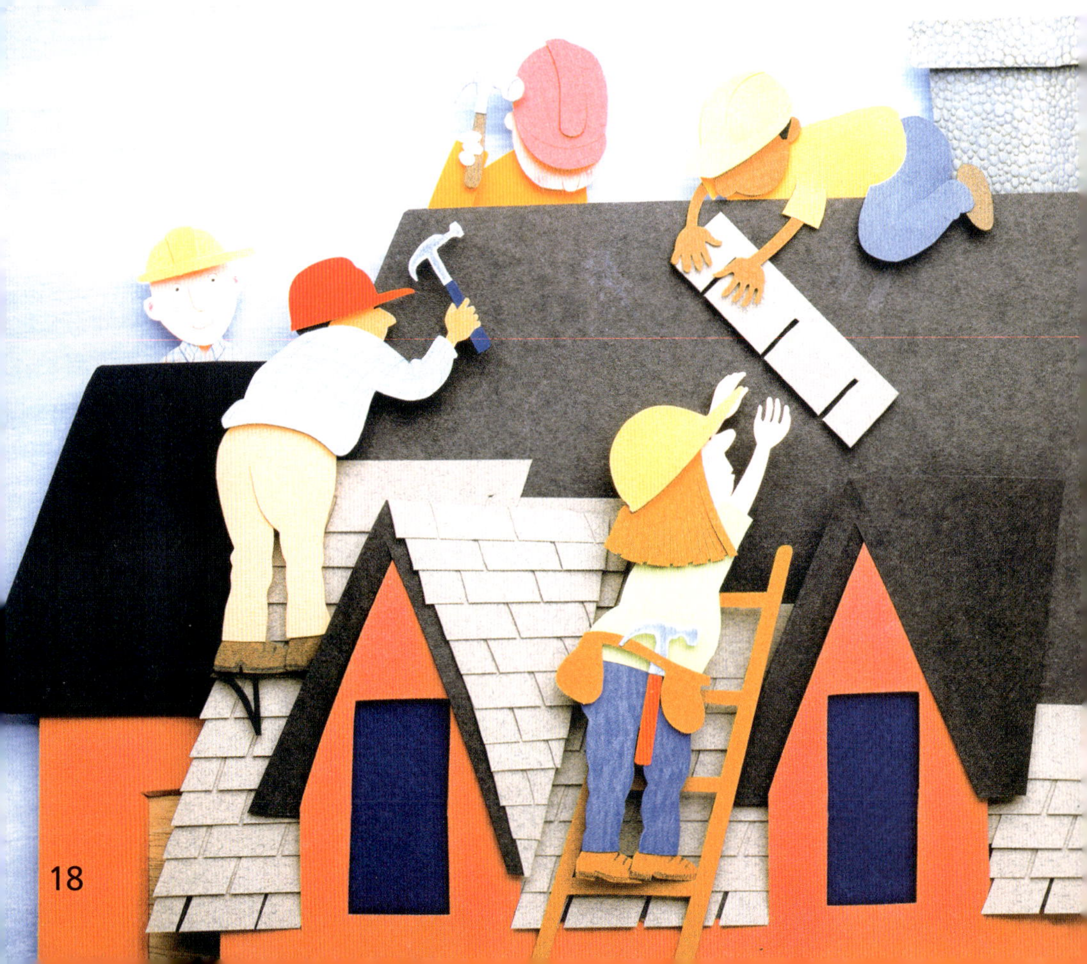

Over in the meadow, with shingles by the drive,
climbed Calvin to the roof with his good roofers **5**.
"Hammer!" said Calvin. "We hammer," said the **5**.
So they hammered on the shingles that were stacked by the drive.

20

Over in the meadow, putting pipes through the floor,
Florence used her wrench and apprentices **4**.
"Plumb!" said Florence. "We plumb," said the **4**.
So they joined all the pipes going through the new floor.

Over in the meadow, testing lights carefully,
wired John the electrician and his trained crew of **3**.
"Connected?" asked John. "Connected!" said the **3**.
So they switched on the power in the house carefully.

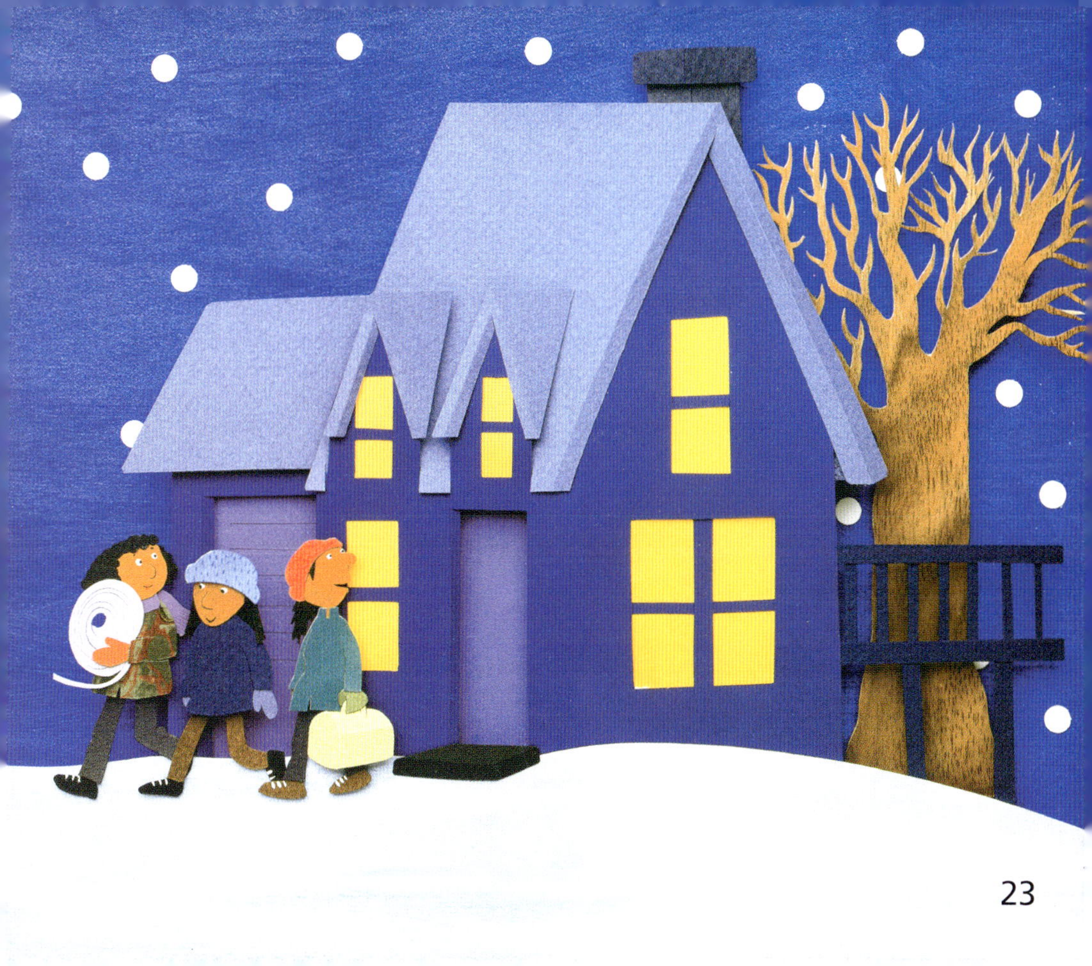

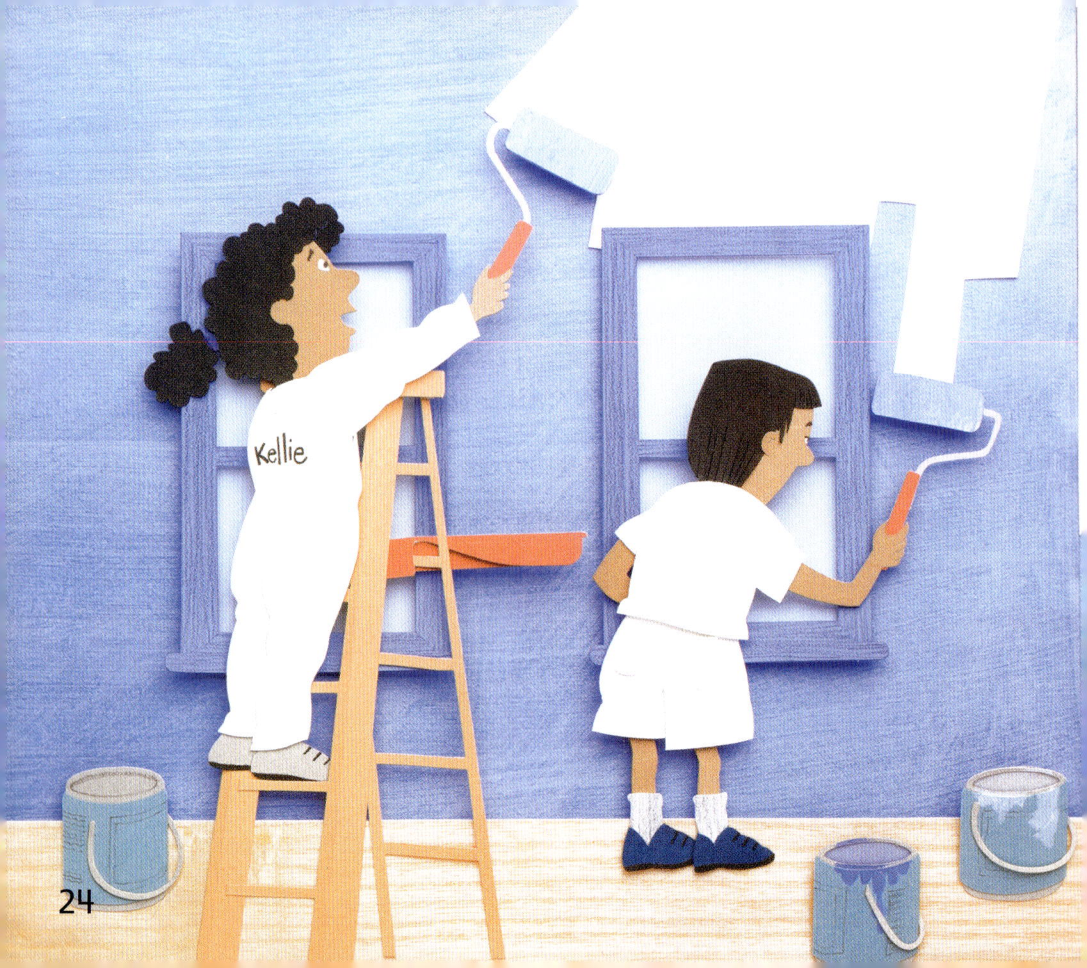
Kellie

Over in the meadow, in the last room to do,
Kellie rolled on paint with her new helpers **2.**
"Use blue," said Kellie. "For the baby!" said the **2.**
So they used the blue paint in the last room to do.

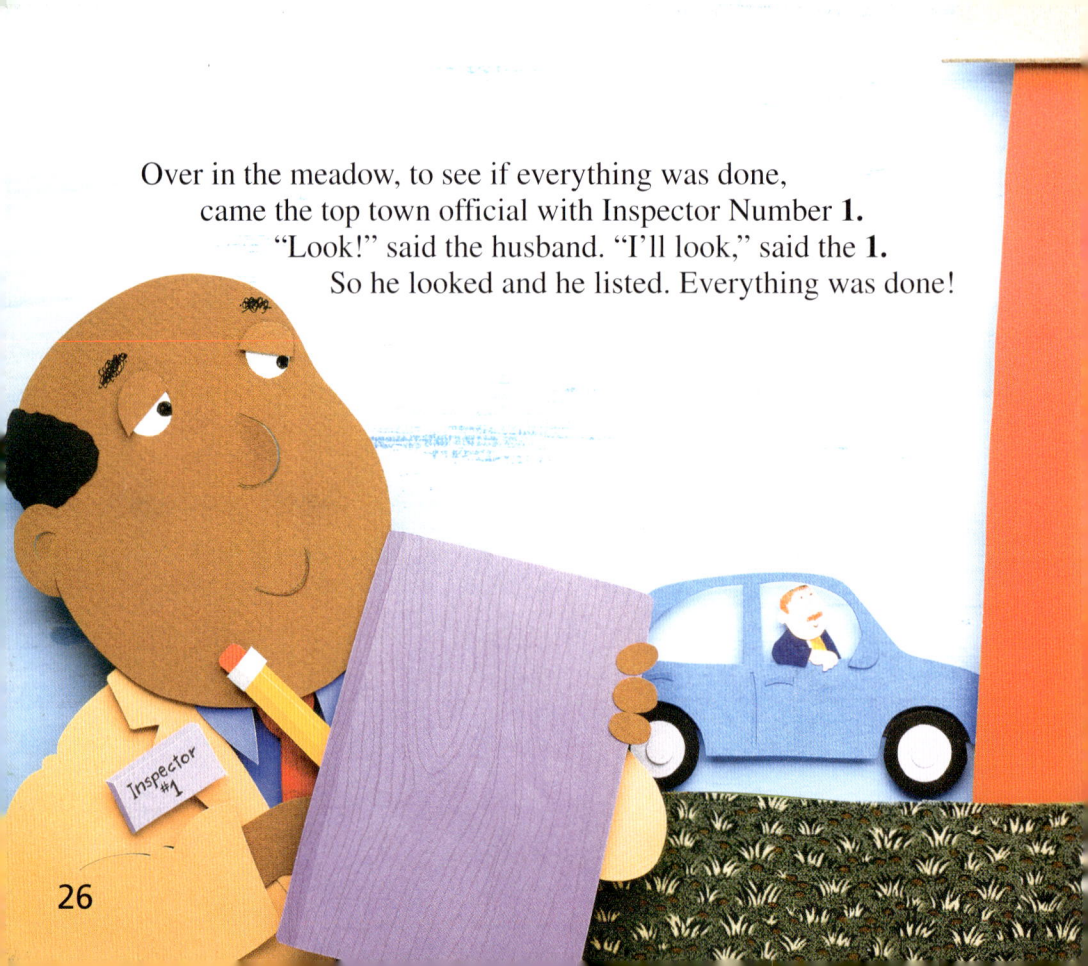

Over in the meadow, to see if everything was done,
came the top town official with Inspector Number **1**.
"Look!" said the husband. "I'll look," said the **1**.
So he looked and he listed. Everything was done!

27

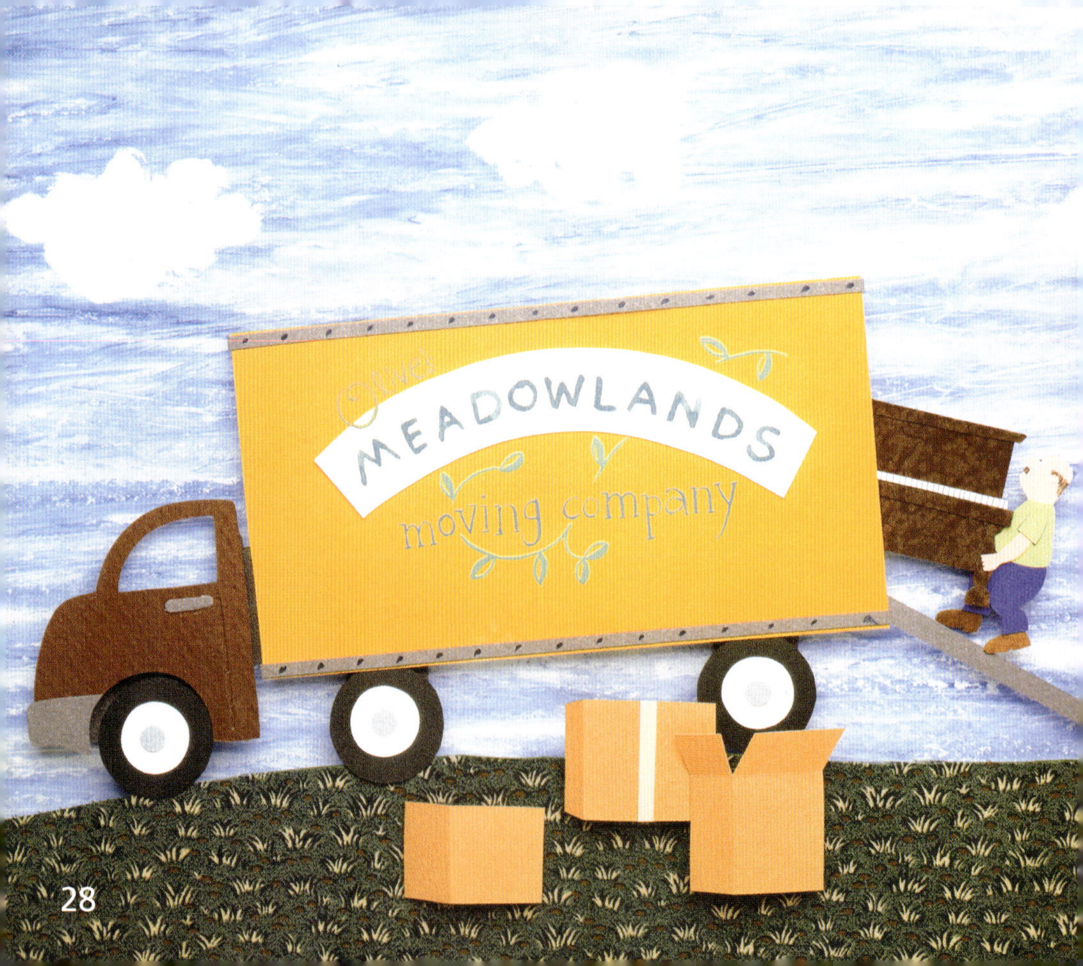

Olive's
MEADOWLANDS
moving company

29

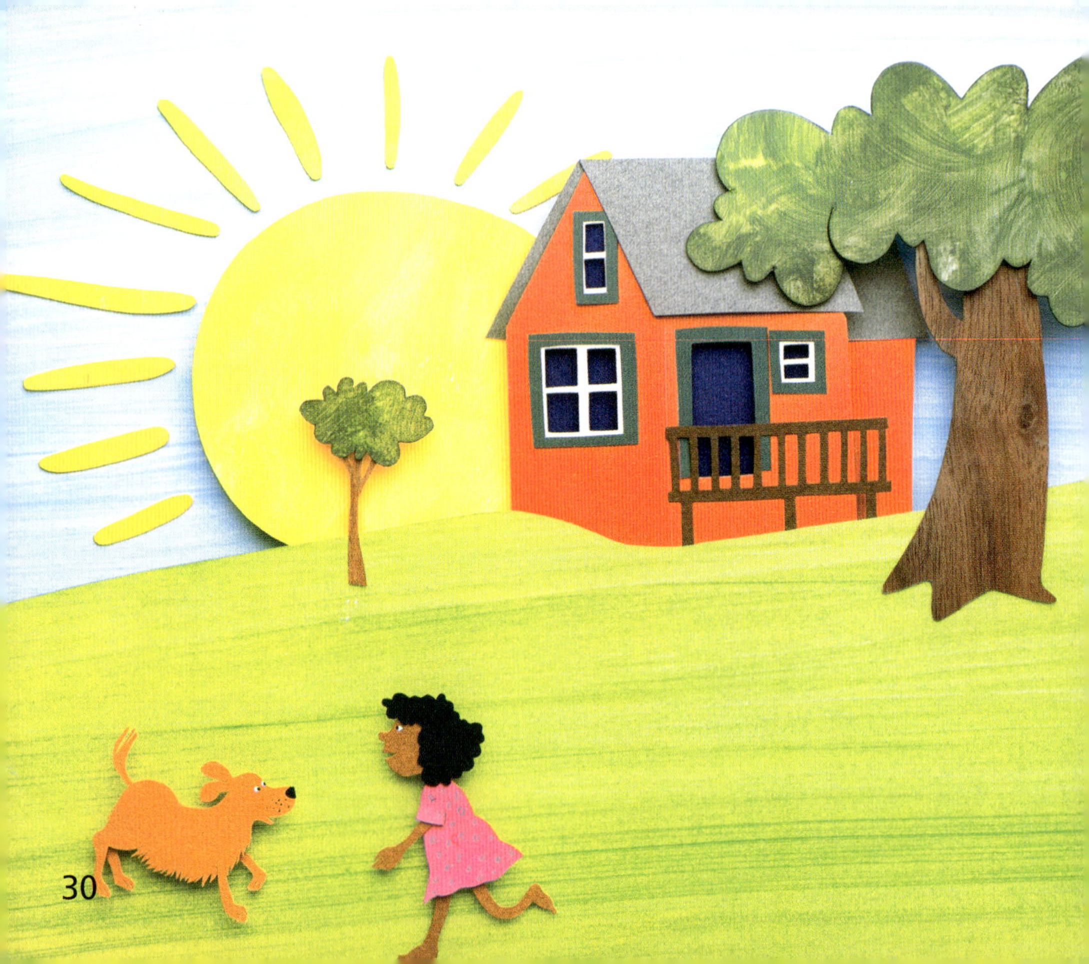

Over in the meadow, by the house, in the sun,
waved the wife and the husband and their new little one.
"Home!" said the couple. "You're home," said everyone.

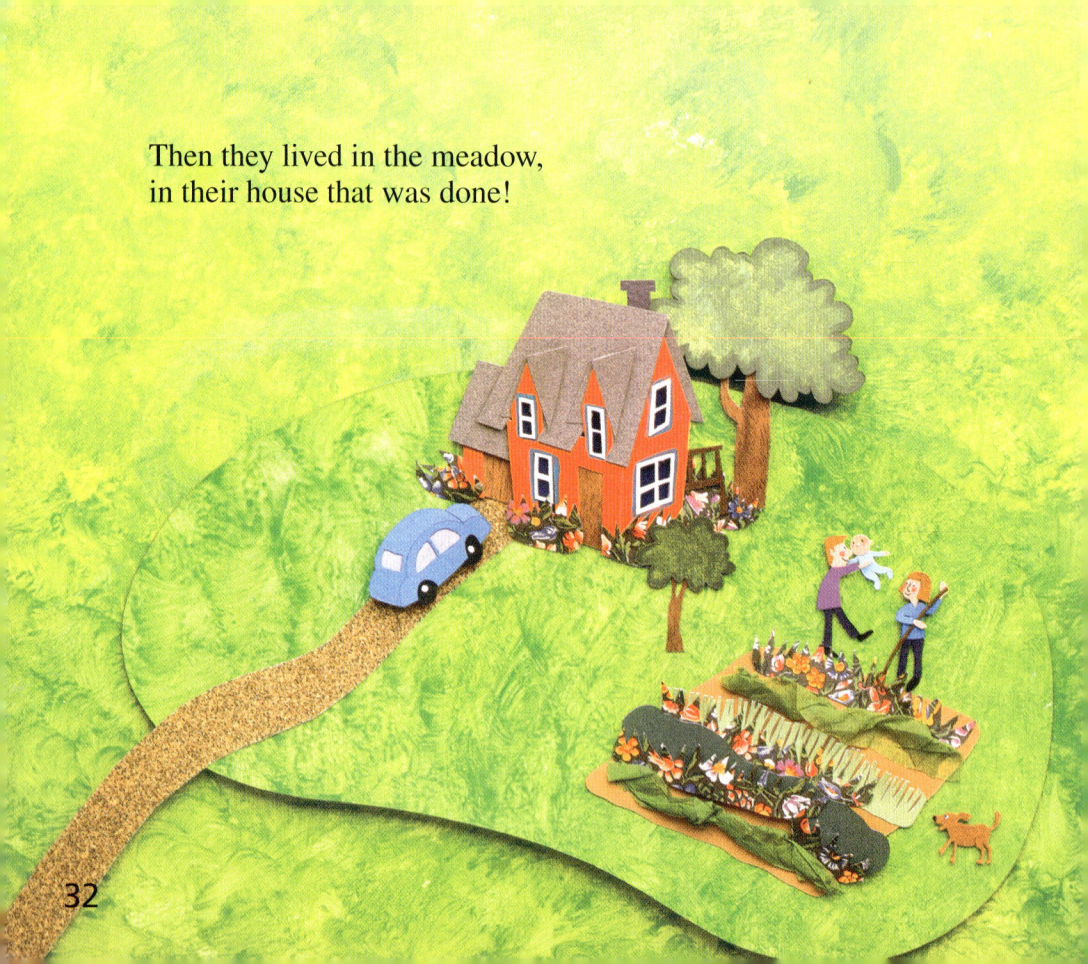

Then they lived in the meadow,
in their house that was done!